500 JOKES FOR GIRLS

PaRragon

Bath • New York • Singapore • Hong Kong • Cologne • Delhi
Melbourne • Amsterdam • Johannesburg • Auckland • Shenzhen

D1397744

This edition published by Parragon in 2012
Parragon
Queen Street House
4 Queen Street
Bath BA1 1HE, UK
www.parragon.com

Copyright © Parragon Books Ltd 2010

ISBN 978-1-4454-6699-6

Printed in China

CONTENTS

Hypnopotamus and
Blubber Gum.............4

Practical Yolks and
Scary Brews...........21

Laughing Stock and
Cross Porpoises..........44

Scaredy Cats and
Ele-pants..........68

Woolly Mammoths and
Nacho Cheese......92

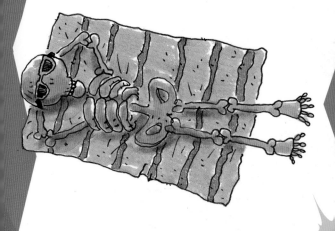

HYPNOPOTAMUS AND BLUBBER GUM

If King Kong went to Hong Kong, played ping-pong, had a sing along and then died, what would they put on his coffin?
A lid.

What's gray and wears glass slippers?
Cinder-elephant!

Why is it easy to cheat a sheep?
Because you can just pull the wool over its eyes.

Why doesn't Sweden export cattle?

Because it wants to keep its Stockholm.

What did the nut say when it sneezed?

'Ca-shew!'

Why couldn't the whales make themselves understood to the angry porpoises?

They were speaking at cross porpoises.

What did Noah do to pass the time on the Ark?

Fished, but he didn't catch much. He only had two worms.

Have you heard the one about the giant fruit cake?
It's very hard to swallow.

What did the boy banana say to the girl banana?
"You have a lot of appeal."

Why did the doughnut go to the dentist?
He needed a filling.

What do you get if you cross a crocodile with a camera?
A snapshot.

Why were the elephants kicked out of the swimming pool?
Because they kept dropping their trunks in the water.

How is a telephone like a dirty bath?
They both have rings.

When is a huge, hairy monster most likely to get into your house?
When you've left the door open.

What do you get when two peas fight?
Black-eyed peas.

What does a frog say when it sees something great?
'Toadly awesome!'

What did the boy gopher say to the girl gopher?
"I gopher you."

How does a lobster answer the phone?
"Shello?"

What do whales chew?
Blubber gum.

What happened when Nelly the Elephant ran away with the circus?
The police made her bring it back.

What did the duck say when he'd finished shopping?

'Put it on my bill, please!'

Why did the hippo wear red suspenders?

To hold up his red pants.

Where do you find giant snails?

On the end of giants' fingers.

When does a horse talk on the phone?

Whinny wants to.

How do you start a flea race?

One, two, flea, go!

What do you get if you cross a phone with a pair of glasses?

A television.

How does a baboon make phone calls?

He just monkeys around on the line.

Why was the baby ant so confused?

Because all its uncles were ants.

What kind of wine does a skeleton like?

One with plenty of body.

**Why do skeletons
wear heavy coats?**
If they don't, the wind goes
right through them.

**What's a cannibal's
favorite game?**
Swallow the leader.

**Which skeleton was
defeated at the
Battle of Waterloo?**
Napoleon Bonyparts.

**Why didn't the
cannibal like eating
the clown?**
He thought it tasted funny.

What do you call a bee that is always complaining?
A grumble bee.

What do cannibals do to their toughest foes?
Stick them in the microwave until they're tender.

What do skeletons say before the start of a meal?
"Bone appétit."

What animals were last off the Ark?
The elephants, because they took a long time to pack their trunks.

What starts with E, ends with E and only has one letter?

An envelope.

What do you get if dinosaurs have a car crash?

Tyrannosaurus wrecks.

What's big and gray and has trouble with personal hygiene?

A smellephant.

What should you do if you go on a picnic with King Kong?

Give him the biggest bananas.

Why do elephants have trunks?

They'd never fit all their clothes in a suitcase.

What do you get if you hunt bear?

Locked up for indecent exposure.

What do you give an elephant to help it sleep?

Trunkquillizers.

What did the birthday balloon say to the pin?

"Hi, Buster."

How do snails get their shells so shiny?

They use snail polish.

What did the pitcher say to the cup?

"I'll have none of your lip."

What did the window say to the Venetian blind?

"If it weren't for you, it would be curtains for me."

Why are elephants tall, grey and wrinkly?

Because if they were small, white and smooth, they would be aspirins.

Why couldn't prehistoric man send birthday cards?

The stamps kept falling off the rocks.

Why are giraffes so cheap to feed?
A little goes a long way.

What happened to the man who dreamt he was eating a giant marshmallow?
He woke up coughing feathers and found that his pillow was missing.

What kind of music do mummies listen to?
Wrap.

What's the best way to find out an elephant's age?
Check his driver's licence.

Why did the rhino see the movie?

He really enjoyed the book.

How do you get a hippo to the top of an oak tree?

Strap it to an acorn and wait fifty years.

What's big and grey and puts everyone into a trance?

A hypnopotamus.

What are aliens' favorite treats?

Martian-mallows!

Why did the witch wash her broomstick?

She wanted to make a clean sweep of it.

What do you call a cheerful kangaroo?

A hop-timist.

What do golfers eat for lunch?

Club sandwiches.

What does Dracula write on his Christmas cards?

"Best vicious of the season."

Why did the ghost go to see an astrologer?

He wanted to see his horror-scope.

What do you get if you cross a grizzly bear with a wizard?

Hairy Potter.

Why did the sorceress buy a huge mansion?

Because she was so witch.

Why wouldn't the skeleton get a job?

He was bone idle.

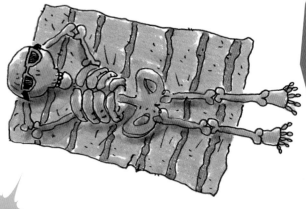

PRACTICAL YOLKS AND SCARY BREWS

What do you get if you cross an alligator with King Midas?

A croc of gold.

Who protects the shores where spirits live?

The ghostguard.

What was the first coffee bar in outer space?

Star-bucks!

What's the largest table in school?

The multiplication table.

Which pets make the most noise?
Trumpets.

Why didn't the hot dog win an Oscar?
Because he didn't get any good rolls.

'Waitress, do you serve crabs?'
'Certainly, sir — we serve anyone.'

How many balls of string would it take to reach the moon?
Just one really long one would do it.

What fly has laryngitis?

A hoarsefly.

What happened to the sardine when it was late for work?

It was canned.

What did the pen say to the paper?

"I dot an 'i' on you."

What do you call a smelly fairy?

Stinkerbell.

Did you hear about the cross-eyed teacher?

He couldn't control his pupils.

What has four wheels and goes, 'Hic! Hic! Hic!'?

A hiccup truck.

What part of a car is the laziest?

The wheels – they're always tired.

What does dirty rain do?

It showers.

What has four eyes and runs for over two thousand miles?

The Mississippi River.

How did the kid catch Egyptian flu?

He caught it from his mummy.

Why did the grandmother put wheels on her rocking chair?

She liked to rock and roll.

Why is a lazy boy nothing like Robinson Crusoe?

Robinson Crusoe got all his work done by Friday.

What did the big chimney say to the little chimney?

"You're too young to smoke!"

What is the best time of year to dig up carrots?
When the farmer is on vacation.

What does a crab use to call someone?
A shellular phone.

What do rabbits do when they get married?
Go on a bunnymoon.

What do you call a dinosaur that never gives up?
A try, try, try-ceratops.

What is a toad's favorite ballet?
Swamp lake.

What animal should you never play cards with?
A cheetah.

How do we know that carrots are good for your eyesight?
Have you ever seen a rabbit wearing glasses?

What do you call a mad sea creature?
A crazy, mixed-up squid.

What colour is a hiccup?
Burple.

What does an educated owl say?
"Who-o-o-m."

Why are orchestras so badly behaved?
They don't know how to conduct themselves.

Why did the monster ask to leave the table?
He'd already eaten the fridge, the stove and the kitchen cabinets.

What's the difference between roast beef and pea soup?

Anyone can roast beef.

Why did the lamp post blush?

It saw the traffic light changing.

What has fifty heads and fifty tails?

Fifty pennies.

How do you know if you've been made upside down?

Your nose runs and your feet smell.

What did one eye say to the other?
"Between us something smells."

What goes around everywhere?
Belts.

Did you hear about the peanuts that walked down a dark alley?
One was assaulted.

What should you say when you meet a ghost?
"How do you boo, sir, how do you boo?"

What tricks do eggs play on each other?
Practical yolks.

What's creamy and chocolaty and can read the future?
Eclair-voyant.

What does a witch's cat say at Halloween?
"Trick or trout?"

Did you hear about the man who tried to cross the Atlantic on a plank of wood?
He couldn't find a plank long enough.

What's the most important program on a witch's computer?

The spell checker.

How do whales communicate?

By sea—mail.

Where do witches have their temples?

Either side of their head.

What's a lion's favorite day of the week?

Chews-day.

What's a parrot's favorite game?

Hide and Speak.

Why couldn't the witch fly for long distances?

She got broomsick.

Why did the wizard get into the fridge?

He was in for a cold spell.

Where does a ghost go on Saturday night?

Anywhere she can boo-gie.

What's the best way to imagine you're flying on a broomstick?

Witchful thinking.

Why didn't the wizard say hello to the twin witches?
He couldn't tell which witch was which.

How can you tell when a window is scared?
It gets shudders.

What do witches take to the beach?
Suntan potion.

What do Hawaiian ghosts play?
The spookulele.

What kind of witch speeds down the highway at 100mph?
A road hag.

Why are little witches at the head of the class?
Because they are so good at spelling.

How should you talk to an evil, ugly witch?
By long-distance phone call.

What do you get if you cross a cocker spaniel, a poodle and a ghost?
A cocker-poodle-boo.

What's Dracula's favorite TV show?

Fiends.

Why is the air so fresh and clean at Halloween?

Because of all the witches sweeping the sky.

What's the difference between a deer on the run and a miniature witch?

One's a hunted stag and the other's a stunted hag.

What's a ghost's favorite dessert?

I scream.

What do ghosts play when they're bored?

Moanopoly.

How do you get rid of a ghost in your house?

Demand he shares the rent.

Why don't witches get angry when they're on a broomstick?

They don't want to fly off the handle.

Why did the witch give up fortune-telling?
She couldn't see a future in it.

What monster sits on the end of your finger?
The Bogeyman.

How do you make a witch float?
Get a couple of scoops of ice cream, some lemonade and a witch.

How can you make a witch scratch?
Take away the 'w'.

What is Dracula's favorite fruit?
Neck-tarines.

What did the congregation say when the witch came down the aisle?

"Here come the bride and broom!"

Where do ghost trains stop?

At manifestations.

What do you call a snowman in the Sahara desert?

A puddle.

Why do ghosts always hang around in threes?

Because two's company, three's a shroud.

Why did the woman spend day and night learning how to cast spells?

She wanted to get witch quick.

What do you call a maggoty corpse with nothing to do?
Bored stiff.

What do near sighted ghosts wear?
Spooktacles or a moanocle.

What rides do ghosts like to go on at the carnival.
The scary-go-round and the roller-ghoster.

What do you get if you cross an ugly witch with a clown?
A scary brew-ha-ha.

Who wrote the novel Spooked Out'?
Terry Fied.

Why was the weather witch so unpopular?
She was always forecasting sunny spells.

Why do witches fly on broomsticks?
Because vacuum cleaners are so heavy.

What's worse than finding a maggot in your apple?
Finding half a maggot in your apple.

What do you call a haunted chicken?
A poultry-geist.

What does a witch wear in the summer?

Open-toad sandals.

What do you call a mysterious wizard on a broomstick?

An unidentified flying sorcerer.

What did the teacher witch do to her terrible student?

Ex-spelled her.

LAUGHING STOCK AND CROSS PORPOISES

What's purple on the outside and green on the inside?

The Incredible Hulk wearing purple pajamas.

Why did the safari guide lose his driving licence?

He parked on a yellow lion.

What do you call a bear with no ear?

A 'b'.

Why can you never swindle a snake?

Because it's impossible to pull its leg.

What does it tell you when you see three polar bears walking down the street wearing blue sweatshirts?

They're all on the same team.

What do you call a terrified dinosaur?

Nervous Rex.

Why do woolly mammoths have trunks?

Because they would look silly with glove compartments.

Did you hear about the cat that swallowed a ball of yarn?
She had mittens.

Why can't skeletons play music in church?
They have no organs.

What did the bald man say when he got a comb for his birthday?
"Thanks, I'll never part with it."

Why did the clock get angry?
It was wound up.

What's the difference between a mosquito and a fly?
A mosquito can fly, but a fly can't mosquito.

What do you call a parrot wearing a raincoat?
Polly unsaturated.

What do you call spending the afternoon with a cranky rabbit?
A bad hare day.

What do you get when you drop a piano down a mineshaft?
A-flat minor.

What kind of tie does a pig wear?
A pig's tie.

What's the best time to go to the dentist?
Two thirty (Tooth hurty).

What do you get if you cross a woolly mammoth with a whale?

A submarine with a built-in snorkel.

What do penguins wear when it's cold?

Ice caps.

What would happen if worms took over the planet?

Global worming.

Why don't penguins carry fish in their pockets?

Because they don't have pockets.

Why are penguins popular on the Internet?

Because they have web feet.

What's a dog's favorite food?

Anything that's on your plate.

Why did the boy try to take his nose apart in winter?

He wanted to see what made it run.

Why are penguins good race car drivers?

Because they're always in pole position.

What do you call a gigantic polar bear?

Nothing, you just run away.

Where do penguins keep their money?

In the snow bank.

What kind of man doesn't like to sit in front of the fire?

The Abominable Snowman.

Why was the pelican kicked out of the hotel?
Because he had a big bill.

Where does money fall like snow?
Wherever there's a change in the weather.

What do you get if you cross a abominable snowman with a kangaroo?
A fur coat with big pockets.

What do you call a abominable snowman in a phone booth
Stuck.

How did the abominable snowman feel when he had flu?

Abominable.

Where do polar bears come from?

Chilly.

What animal talks too much?

A yak.

What do abominable snowman call their offspring?

Chill-dren.

How do robins get in shape?
They do worm-ups.

What is brown, has a hump and lives at the North Pole?
A very lost camel.

Name six things smaller than an ant's mouth.
Six of its teeth.

What do you call angry dolphins?
Cross porpoises.

What do cows do on Saturday nights?
Go to the mooooooovies.

Where do horses go when they are sick?
To the horsepital.

What's big, black and eats polar bears?
A big, black polar bear eater.

What did the boy octopus say to the girl octopus?
"I want to hold your hand, hand, hand, hand, hand, hand, hand, hand."

What did the scientist say when he found bones on the moon?

"The cow didn't make it."

What kind of car does a cat drive?

A Cat-a-lac.

What's the difference between a piano and a fish?

You can tune a piano, but you can't tuna fish.

What do sharks eat with their peanut butter?
Jellyfish.

What did one casket say to the other casket?
"Is that you coffin?"

What do you get if you cross a duck with a rooster?
A bird that wakes you up at the quack of dawn.

What happens when a faucet, a dog and a tomato run a race?
Well, the dog is in the lead, the faucet is running and the tomato is trying to catch up.

Why can't Cinderella play football?

Because she always runs away from the ball.

Where do monkeys make toast?

Under a gorilla.

What do you get if you cross a chocolate bar with an elk?

A chocolate mousse.

What do you get if you sit under a cow?

A pat on the head.

Where do tough chickens come from?

Hard-boiled eggs.

What do you call a camel with no humps?

Humphrey.

What says "quick, quick"?

A duck with hiccups.

How do mountains hear?

They have mountaineers.

What do nuclear scientists like to eat?

Fission chips.

What's a pirate's favorite subject?
Arrrr-t!

What did the zero say to the eight?
"Nice belt."

What's black and white and read all over?
A newspaper.

What did the traffic light say to the car?
"Don't look now, I'm changing."

What would you do if you broke your leg in two places?
Stay away from those places in future.

Why did the snowman die with his boots on?
Because he didn't want to stub his toe when he kicked the bucket.

What do you get if you cross a polar bear with a flower?
I don't know, but I'm not going to smell it.

Have you ever seen a man-eating polar bear?
No, but in a diner I once saw a man eating chicken.

Why was the seal swimming the backstroke?
It had just had lunch and didn't want to swim on a full stomach.

Is it better to write with your right or left hand?
Ideally, you should be writing with a pen, not a hand.

Do moths cry?
Sure. Haven't you ever seen a moth bawl?

Why did the stupid boy wear a turtleneck sweater?

To hide his flea collar.

What happens if you throw a red ruby in the Black Sea?

It gets wet.

What do you get if you cross a chemical with a bicycle?

Bike carbonate of soda.

Why did the farmer plough his field with a steamroller?

He wanted to grow mashed potatoes.

What did the big weevil say to the little weevil?

"You're the lesser of two weevils."

Can you spell eighty in two letters?

A T.

Why do giraffes have such long necks?

Because their feet smell.

Why did the skunk take an aspirin?
Because it had a stinking cold.

Why is a shirt with eight buttons so interesting?
Because you fasten eight (fascinate).

Why did the coffee taste like mud?
Because it was ground that morning.

What do you do if you split your sides laughing?
Run till you get a stitch.

When are most frogs born?
In a leap year.

What do you get if you cross a toad with a galaxy?
Star Warts.

How does Luke Skywalker get from planet to planet?
Ewoks (He walks).

Why do rabbits eat rust?
Because it's a type of car rot.

What does a dentist call his X-rays?
Tooth pics.

What do you get hanging from trees in the jungle?
Sore arms.

What happened to the man who couldn't tell the difference between soap and putty?
His armpits stuck together and all his windows fell out.

How do you make a lemon drop?
Let go of it.

How can you make seven even?
Take away the letter 's'.

SCAREDY CATS AND ELE-PANTS

How do ghosts like their eggs?
Terrifried.

What do you call a sorceress waiting by the roadside with her thumb out?
A witchhiker.

Why don't witches fly around on vacuum cleaners?
They can't find long enough extension cord.

What is evil and warty on the inside, and pink and fluffy on the outside?

A witch dressed as a furry pig.

What kind of pets do ghosts have?

Scaredy cats.

What kind of music do ghosts like?

Haunting melodies.

Where do foreign ghosts live?

In a distant terror-tory.

Where did the ghosts live in the Wild West?
Tombstone.

What has six legs and flies?
A witch and her cat on a broomstick.

What do you get if you cross a bear with a skunk?
Winnie the Pooh.

What do you give a sick canary?
Tweetment.

Why do hummingbirds hum?
Because they don't know the words.

Why did the skeleton call off the wedding?

His heart wasn't in it.

What do you call a stupid skeleton?

Bonehead.

How did the sick witch get to hospital?

She flu.

What do cannibals eat for dessert?

Chocolate-covered aunts.

Why didn't the skeleton go bungee-jumping?

He didn't have the guts.

Why was the cannibal expelled from school?

He kept buttering up the teacher.

Why did the skeleton go to jail?

He was bad to the bone.

Why are skeletons so calm?

Because nothing gets under their skin.

What is Beethoven doing in his coffin right now?

Decomposing.

What kind of art do skeletons rave about?
Skullture.

How does a skeleton stop?
Vertebrakes.

What are the biggest ants in the world?
Giants.

How do you attract King Kong?
Hang upside down in a tree and make a noise like a banana.

What's a ghost's favorite ice-cream flavor?
Shock-olate chip.

What do you get if you cross a very bent piece of wood with a spaceship?

Warp factor nine.

When can three giant dinosaurs get under an umbrella and not get wet?

When it isn't raining.

What are the second biggest ants in the world?

Elephants.

What's green, very tall and mopes in the corner?

The incredible sulk.

How do dinosaurs pass exams?

With extinction.

What weighs two tons and sticks to the roof of your mouth?
Peanut butter and rhino sandwiches.

What do you get if King Kong sits on your piano?
A flat note.

Why did the hippo put on a yellow wig?
To see if blondes have more fun.

What do you get if you cross a telephone with a ghost?
A phantom caller.

What do you get if you cross a rhino with a spider?
A rhino that has trouble getting out of your bath.

What's the best time of year to see a man-eating tiger?
I don't know – but at Christmas, it's easy to see a man eating turkey.

Why don't elephants use computers?

They're afraid of the mouse.

What do you get if you cross a telephone with a dog?

A golden receiver.

What does a triceratops sit on?

Its tricera-bottom.

What do you get if you cross a dinosaur with Eminem?

A rap-tor!

Why did the fat monster put a candle on his tummy?

He was celebrating his girthday.

What do you call a gorilla with bananas in its ears?

Anything you like, it can't hear you.

What happened to the elephant that had too much whisky?

It got trunk.

What's big, strong, green and very tough to chew?

The Inedible Hulk.

What is an elf's favorite kind of birthday cake?
Shortcake.

What do grizzlies take with them on vacation.
Just the bear essentials.

What do giants tell each other?
Tall stories.

When do tigers eat people?
Chewsdays.

What's Nelly the Elephant's middle name?
The.

What do you call a woman with a sheep on her head?

Baa-baa-ra.

How many people can fit into the world's largest stadium when it's empty?

One – after that, it's no longer empty.

Why couldn't the skunk use her phone?

It was out of odour.

What's the best way to prevent infection from a polar bear bite?
Don't bite any polar bears.

How do you get a rhino out of a phone booth?
The same way you got him in.

Why did the elephant leave the circus?
He was fed up with working for peanuts.

How can you tell if someone with curly hair is on the phone?
You get a frizzy signal.

What's the biggest prehistoric insect?
The mam-moth.

What's the difference between a hippo and a banana?

Try picking it up – if you can't, it's either a hippo or a giant banana.

What should you do if a rhino charges?

Pay it and run.

Why do dogs wag their tails?

Because no on else will do it for them.

What newspaper do cows read?

The Daily Moos.

Why did the giant have a pocket calculator?

To work out how many pockets he had.

Why did the big game hunter stop hunting elephants?

He got tired of carrying around the decoys.

What did the jack say to the car?

"Can I give you a lift?"

What did the big ape say when he dialled incorrectly?

"Oops. King Kong ring wrong."

Why do hippos wear sandals?

Otherwise they would sink into the sand.

Why is Ireland so rich?

Because its capital is always Dublin.

How do we know that peanuts are fattening?

Have you ever seen a skinny elephant eating peanuts?

What do you get if you cross a cow with a goat?

Butter from a butter.

What happens when ghosts haunt a theater?

The actors get stage fright.

What do you call a voodoo elephant?
Mumbo jumbo.

Why did cavemen draw pictures of rhinoceroses and hippopotamuses?
It was much easier than spelling their names.

What do lions say before they start hunting?
"Let us prey."

Why do hippos wallow in mud?
They think it's slick.

What's the difference between African and Indian elephants?

About three thousand miles.

What do you call a dog with a cold?

A choo-wawa.

What do you call a bee born in May?

A maybe.

What's big and red and lies upside down in the gutter?

A dead bus.

What's the best way to get King Kong begging on his knees?
Wave a four-ton banana in front of his nose.

Why did the doll blush?
Because she saw the teddy bear.

What do you get if you cross a computer with a ballet?
The Nutcracker Suite.

What has wings, a long tail and wears a bow?
A birthday pheasant.

Is it hard to bury an elephant?
Yes, it's a huge undertaking.

How can you tell a male dinosaur from a female dinosaur?

Ask a question and if he answers, it's male, but if she answers, it's female.

How do you take a lion's temperature?

Very carefully.

What sort of fish would you find in a shoe?

An eel.

Why do elephants have flat feet?

From jumping off tall trees.

Why do windows squeak when you open them?

Because they have panes.

How much did the fish weigh?

It was off the scales.

What are you if you step into a cowpat?

An incowpoop.

What does a ghost call his mum and dad?

Transparents.

What did the ghost say after he had been out haunting all night?

"I'm dead on my feet."

What do you get if you cross a witch's cat with a lemon?
A sour puss.

What did the bat say to the witch's hat?
"You go on ahead and I'll hang around."

What do you call a nervous witch?
A twitch.

Who do ghosts invite to their parties?
Polterguests.

WOOLLY MAMMOTHS AND NACHO CHEESE

Why can't woolly mammoths ride bicycles?

Because they don't have thumbs to ring the bell.

How do fish go into business?

They start on a small scale.

How did the scorpion story end?

There was a sting in the tale.

How do you describe the average cannibal?

A guy with a wife and ate children.

What do you call a fly with no wings?

A walk.

What did the grapes say when the monks stepped on them?

Nothing – they just let out a little whine.

To whom do fish go to borrow money?

The loan shark.

Which reindeer have the shortest legs?

The smallest ones.

How many woolly mammoths does it take to screw in a light bulb?
Two, but you need a really big light bulb.

If athletes get athlete's foot what do astronauts get?
Mistle toe.

What did the cannibal do when he saw an all-you-can-eat restaurant?
He ate all the customers.

What's the coldest creature in the sea?
A blue whale.

How did the Vikings send secret messages?

By norse code.

Did you hear about the cannibal who came home late for dinner?

His wife gave him an evil eye.

What do you get if you cross an alligator with a stomach upset?

An illigator.

How do penguins drink?

Out of beak-ers.

Who has large antlers and wears white gloves?
Mickey Moose.

What's worse than raining cats and dogs?
Hailing taxis.

Where do fish wash?
In a river basin.

What do reindeer have that no other animals have?
Baby reindeer.

What happens after a dry spell?
It rains.

What's a penguin's favourite salad?
Iceberg lettuce.

Who's the penguin's favourite aunt?
Aunt-arctica.

How does a penguin make pancakes?
With his flippers.

What kind of tree is hairy?
A fur tree.

What happens to a reindeer when it stands out in the rain?

It gets wet.

Could you kill the Abominable Snowman just by throwing eggs at him?

Of course – he'd be eggs-terminated.

Why shouldn't you dance with a abominable snowman?

Because you might get flat feet.

Why was the Abominable Snowman's dog named Frost?

Because Frost bites.

What did the Abominable Snowman do after he had his teeth pulled out?

He ate the dentist – whole!

What is the Abominable Snowman's favorite book?

'War and Frozen Peas'.

What do birds give out on Halloween?

Tweets.

What did one abominable snowman say to the other?

"I'm afraid I just don't believe in people."

What did the snowball do when it stopped rolling?

Looked round.

How do you stop a dog barking in the back seat of a car?

Put him in the front seat.

What side of a turkey do the feathers grow on?

The outside.

When is the Arctic Ocean like a piece of string?
When a ship makes knots in it.

What's the difference between a dog and a painter?
One sheds his coat and the other coats his shed.

What kind of dog tells the time?
A watchdog.

What do you use to cut through giant waves?
A sea-saw.

How do you stop a rhino from charging?

Take away its credit card.

What do you call a cow that has just had a baby?

Decalfinated.

Why can't a leopard hide?

Because he's always spotted.

Where are there no fat people?

In Finland.

What goes 99-thump, 99-thump, 99-thump?

A centipede with a wooden leg.

How do rabbits mail letters?
By haremail.

When is a painting like a can of sardines?
When it's done in oils.

Why did the chewing gum cross the road?
Because it was stuck to the chicken's foot.

What do you call a box of fifty ducks?
A box of quackers.

Why did the chicken cross the playground?
To get to the other slide.

What did one firefly say to the other when his light went out?
"Give me a push, my battery is dead."

What sort of drink would you get from a polar bear?
Iced tea.

"Doctor, Doctor! I think I've swallowed a ten dollar bill"
"Come back tomorrow and we'll see if there's any change."

'Your socks have got holes in them!'

'How else would I get my feet in?'

Why are monsters so smart?

Because two heads are better than one.

How do you know which end of a worm is its head?

Tickle it and see which end laughs.

What did one candle say to the other candle?

"Shall we go out tonight?"

Why is six afraid of seven?

Because seven ate nine.

Why are sausages bad mannered?

Because they spit in the frying pan.

How are monsters and moms alike?

They both have eyes in the back of their heads.

What do you get if you cross a cat with a parrot?

A carrot.

What is white and goes up?
A confused snowflake.

What do you call a cat at the beach?
Sandy Claws.

What lies at the bottom of the Arctic Sea and shivers?
A nervous wreck.

What story do little ghosts like to hear at bedtime?
'Ghouldilocks and the Three Scares'.

Why didn't the husky dog speak to his foot?
Because it's not polite to talk back to your paw.

How do you stop a cold getting to your chest?
Tie a knot in your neck.

What do you call a spaceship with its exhaust pipe hanging off?
A space racket.

Why did the festering zombie stay in bed?
He felt rotten.

How does a broom act?
With sweeping gestures.

What does a unicorn call its father?
Popcorn.

What did the musician say to the audience?
Ear we go again.

What grows between your nose and your chin?
Two lips.

What do comets say to each other when they meet?
"Glad to meteor!"

Why was the musician arrested?
He was always getting into treble.

What goes in pink and comes out blue?

A swimmer on a cold day.

What do you call a chicken crossing the road?

Poultry in motion.

Why did Julius Caesar buy crayons?

He wanted to Mark Antony.

What has a black hat, flies on a broomstick and can't see?

A witch with her eyes closed.

What did the nose say to the boy?

'Why are you always picking on me?'

What goes "Oooooo"?

A cow with no lips.

Why is a mouse like hay?

Because the cat'll (cattle) eat it.

What shoes do you make from banana skins?

Slippers.

Where do astronauts keep their sandwiches?
In a launch box.

Why does a lion kneel before it springs?
Because it is preying.

What kind of driver doesn't need a licence?
A screwdriver.

Did you hear about the man who crossed the Alps twice without taking a shower?
The dirty double-crosser!

What do you get if you cross a cow with a grass cutter?
A lawn mooer.

Where did the pilgrims land when they went to America?
On their feet.

What is a sleeping bag?
A knapsack.

What can you keep even if you give it away?
A cold.

What's the difference between a deadly disease and a Klingon?
One's smallpox and the other mauls Spock.

Why is Saturday night important to Julius's girlfriend?

Because that's when Julius Caesar.

Why do bakers work late?

They knead the dough.

What makes a good librarian?

Shelf control.

What spacious car lives in a French cathedral?

The Hatchback of Notre Dame.

What do you call a cheese that isn't yours?
Nacho cheese.

What do you call a greasy chicken?
A slick chick.

Who drives all his customers away but still makes a living?
A taxi driver.

Why did the girl laugh?
She hit her funny bone.

What do you get if you cross a sports reporter with a vegetable?

A common 'tater.

What do ants use for hula hoops?

Cheerios.

What's the difference between a train and a tree?

One leaves its shed and the other sheds its leaves.

Why is Sunday stronger than Monday?

Because Monday is a weak day.

What Roman numeral can climb a wall?

IV (ivy).

What is everyone's favorite tree?
A poplar tree.

How can you catch dandruff?
Shake your head over a paper bag.

How does Moby Dick celebrate his birthday?
He has a whale of a time.

How many ears does Captain Kirk have?
Three – a left ear, a right ear and a final frontier.

What tool do you use in math class?
Multi-pliers.

Why was the little chimney ill?

It caught flu.

What do you call a Roman emperor with a cold?

Julius Sneezer.

What do you call an amusing horse racer?

A jokey.

What swings through the jungle on vines backwards?

Nazrat.

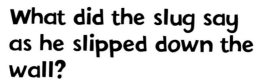

What did the slug say as he slipped down the wall?

How slime flies!

What bus has crossed the Atlantic?

Columbus.

What gets smaller the more you put in it?

A hole.

What did the wall say to the other wall?

"See you at the corner."

What do you call a pen with no hair?
A bald point.

Why are oranges like bells?
They peel.

What's a dimple?
An upside-down pimple.

'Do you always wash in dirty water?'
'It wasn't dirty when I started.'

How can you tell if there's a woolly mammoth under your bed?
Your nose is touching the ceiling.

What's purple and hums?
An electric plum.

What kind of nut do you hang pictures on?
A walnut.

What did one keyboard say to the other keyboard?
"Sorry, you're not my type."

What's green and rocks?
Elvis Parsley.

What's the definition of 'debate'?
It's what lures de fish.

What did the mouse say to the camera?
Cheese.

Where do snowmen put their web pages?
On the winternet.

How can you double your money?
Look at it in a mirror.

What do you call an overweight ET?
An extra cholesterol.

What do you call a abominable snowman that does a hundred sit-ups a day?
The abdominal snowman.

What do you get if you cross a dog with a frog?
A croacker spaniel.

What's the difference between someone who needs to go to the bathroom and someone who's trapped in a lions' den?
One is dying to go and the other is going to die.

Why shouldn't you swim on a full stomach?
It's much easier swimming in a full swimming pool.

When does a ghost have breakfast?

In the moaning.

Why couldn't the ghost go on the bus?

He didn't have the correct chains.

Why do ghosts shiver and moan?

You'd do the same if you had to walk around under a sheet all day.

What do you get if you cross a snake with a pie?

A pie—thon.

Why did the woolly mammoth eat the crazy man?

Someone said he was nuts.

What goes "Cackle, cackle, splat!"?
A witch flying into a lamp post.

What do you call an owl with a toupee?
Hedwig.

What do you get when you cross Bambi with a ghost?
Bamboo.

What trees do witches plant in their gardens?
Brooms.

What goes, "Cackle, cackle, crackle!"?
A witch spontaneously combusting.

What's the difference between a witch and the letters m, a, k, e and s?
One makes spells and the others spell 'makes'.

What do ghosts drink at breakfast?
Coffee with scream and sugar.

What did the mother ghost say to the baby ghost?
"Put your boos and shocks on."

What are a ghoul's best friend?
Demons.

What do ghosts eat for dinner?
Spook-ghetti.

Where do phantoms mail their letters?
At the ghost office.

When do ghosts go to work?
Moandays to Frightdays.

What vehicle does a kid ghost like to ride?
A boocycle.

Why did the witch take a week to make a spell?
It was a slow-motion-potion.

Why don't polar bears buy shoes?
Because when they wear them they still have bear feet.